PRIMARY HANDBOOK
FOR BASSOON
BY RICHARD POLONCHAK

Published By
MEREDITH MUSIC PUBLICATIONS
a division of G.W. Music, Inc.

MEREDITH MUSIC PUBLICATIONS and its stylized double M logo are trademarks
of MEREDITH MUSIC PUBLICATIONS, a division of G.W. Music, Inc.

Book layout by Capital Music Service
Cover design by John Heinly
Illustrations by Elizabeth A. Schaefer

ISBN: 1-57463-052-0

First Edition
June 1982

PRIMARY HANDBOOK FOR BASSOON

Preface

PRIMARY HANDBOOK FOR BASSOON is both a source manual and comprehensive bassoon method written especially for music teachers who must teach the bassoon but who are not bassoonists themselves. As a teaching method, this book is designed to take a student from beginning to advanced high school level. As a college text, this book will provide the woodwind methods student with a thorough background in both the teaching and the playing aspects of the bassoon.

In this handbook, much attention has been given to the "externals" of bassoon playing (care and maintenance, hand positions, embouchure, reeds, etc.) because they are so crucial to the student's success. While the bulk of this material is found in the "Introduction," various "Instrument Checks" are also found throughout the text. These checks are procedures to find out if certain mechanisms on the bassoon are in proper working order. The "checks" are presented as the new notes that depend on such mechanisms are introduced. The "Instrument Checks" point out *what the ideal should be;* they are not presented as a repair guide. A bassoon technician or reputable repair facility will be able to facilitate corrections.

The fingerings are presented in a manner that relates them to other woodwind instruments with the keys being named by the notes that they produce. Resonance and intonation corrections are circled. These "corrections" are additional keys that can be added if needed to correct intonation and/or resonance problems. Professional bassoonists use expensive instruments that often may not need much "correction" to the notes. However, the instruments found in schools are usually not of this caliber and, therefore, will often need the corrections presented.

Over fifteen years of teaching junior high, high school and college-level bassoon students have led to the methods and techniques found in this handbook. Musical exercises are presented in a logical sequence emphasizing a good foundation. For example, the student begins with both hands on the bassoon for two reasons: (1) proper position and instrument support are established immediately and (2) the notes played by both hands use much less "lip pressure" so that by the time the student reaches notes using just one or two tone holes, the lips can be "built-up" to handle them. To complete this method successfully will require some time. The musical material is *not* "reading" material; it is meant to be learned well before going on. Teachers desiring additional "drill-type" materials can easily find many such exercises to add to this book. Also, when used in a teaching situation, PRIMARY HANDBOOK FOR BASSOON is not a self-instruction book for students. While many facets of bassoon playing are explained in detail, the teacher is needed to clarify what is *not* explained. All of the teacher's musical background and knowledge must be added to this manual for its total success.

My special thanks go to two persons who have been inspirations to me as a bassoonist: Mr. Benjamin Spiegel (Pittsburgh Symphony/Duquesne University) who taught me to play the bassoon and to make reeds. Many of his ideas, methods, and philosophies have found their way into this book; and Mr. Lewis Hugh Cooper (Detroit Symphony/University of Michigan) who has taught me so much about the design and maintenance of the bassoon.

It is my sincere hope that PRIMARY HANDBOOK FOR BASSOON will provide an enjoyable approach for those who learn and for those who teach the bassoon.

RMP
Alexandria, Virginia

To my wife, Cathy Ann, for loving presence.

Fingering Chart for German System Bassoon

by

Richard M. Polonchak

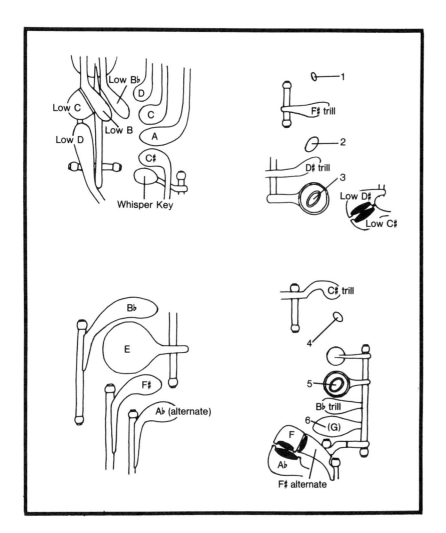

1. When two fingerings are given, the first one is the primary fingering and the second one is the alternate fingering.

2. The third tone hole of the right hand is really the G Key (see diagram at left.)

3. The keys are named for the notes they produce. "L" stands for "Low." "W" refers to "Whisper Key."

4. ● = "Half-Hole" and refers to a partially-opened tone hole. While it is usually opened halfway, it could be more or less than half depending on the particular note and bassoon in question. The finger "rolls" down to open the hole.

5. Some bassoons do not have the High D Key. Also, the G trill (High E) and D♯ trill are optional on many bassoons.

6. The circled fingerings indicate the optional keys to be added if needed to improve intonation and/or resonance.

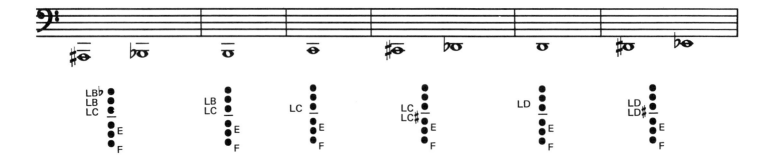

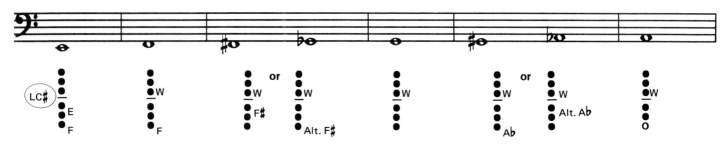

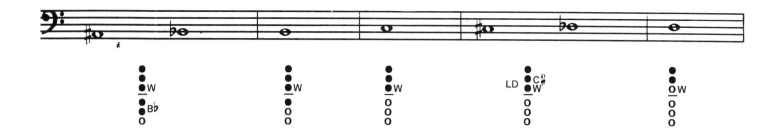

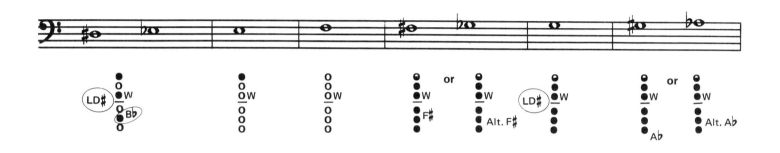

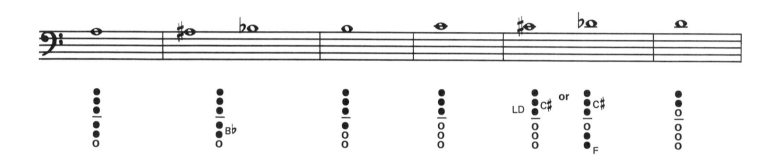

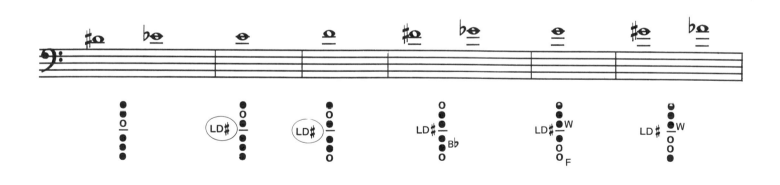

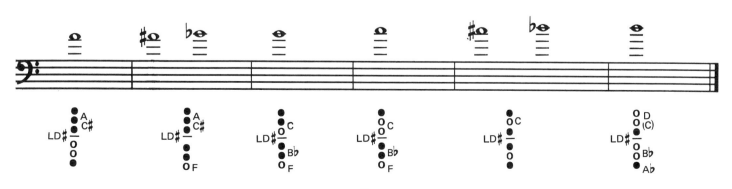

5

Introduction

Assembling the Bassoon

Note: Never force the sections of the bassoon together. Tenons that are too tight must be lubricated. Figure 1 shows a tenon. Cork Tenons—use Vaseline or cork grease to lubricate. Threaded Tenons—use paraffin wax or beeswax to lubricate; never use cork grease or Vaseline as they will cause the thread to rot!

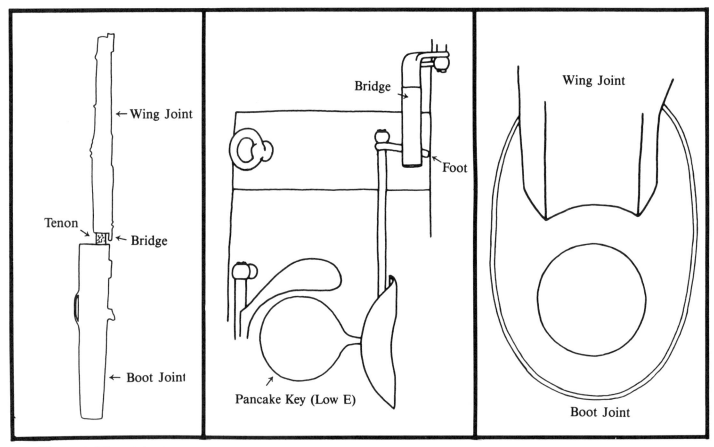

| Figure 1. Wing Joint into Boot Joint | Figure 2. Bridge over Pancake Key | Figure 3. Concentric Circles |

1. Hold the Boot Joint in the right hand with the Pancake Key facing you (See the key diagram on the Fingering Chart, page 4). The Low E Key is called the Pancake Key because it looks like a pancake.

2. Hold the Wing Joint in the left hand and depress the Whisper Key to raise the bridge (Figure 1).

3. Twist the Wing Joint into the smaller hole on the Boot Joint so the bridge fits over the foot of the Pancake Key (Figure 2). The inner curve of the Wing Joint should be *concentric* to the larger hole on the Boot Joint (Figure 3).

4. Pick up the Bass Joint in the left hand and twist it into the larger hole on the Boot Joint. Then "lock" the Wing and Bass Joints together so that they are stable (Figure 4). To "lock" the sections together, slide the Joint Lock Pin on the Bass Joint into its receiver on the Wing Joint. If your bassoon does not have a Joint Lock, position the Bass Joint so that the keys are close to the Wing Joint and so that the keys on both sections form a "flat table of keys" when put together. A Joint Lock should be added to bassoons without one. The Lock makes the sections stable and protects the vulnerable tenons.

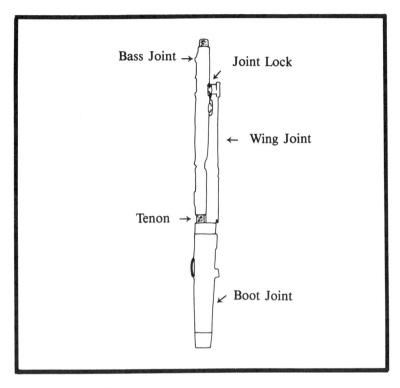

Figure 4. Bass Joint into Boot Joint.

5. Take the Bell in the left hand. Hold the B♭ down on the Bell and twist onto the Bass Joint (Figure 5). The B♭ key is positioned over the arm of the long key on the Bass Joint that extends over the tenon.
6. Hold the bocal in the right hand as shown in Figure 6 and, while exerting a *slight* downward force, *twist the bassoon* so that the bocal slides in the Wing Joint. The small hole in the vent of the bocal must fall under the Whisper Key pad.

Note: If your bassoon has a Whisper Key Lock (the left-hand lock is mounted under the Whisper Key on the Wing Joint/the right-hand lock is mounted on the Boot Joint near the C♯ Trill Key), this lock must be in the "off" position in order to put the bocal in the bassoon.

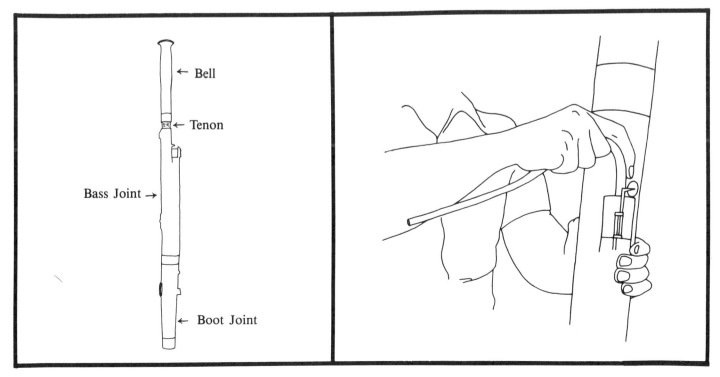

Figure 5. Bass Joint to Bell.   **Figure 6. Bocal into Wing Joint.**

Supporting the Bassoon

In America, the preferred method of supporting the bassoon is with a seatstrap. In Europe, the neckstrap and hand-crutch are used. By using a seatstrap, the bassoon becomes weightless. The strap fits *diagonally* across the chair (Figure 7) and hooks into the small hole at the bottom of the Boot Joint cap (Figure 8).

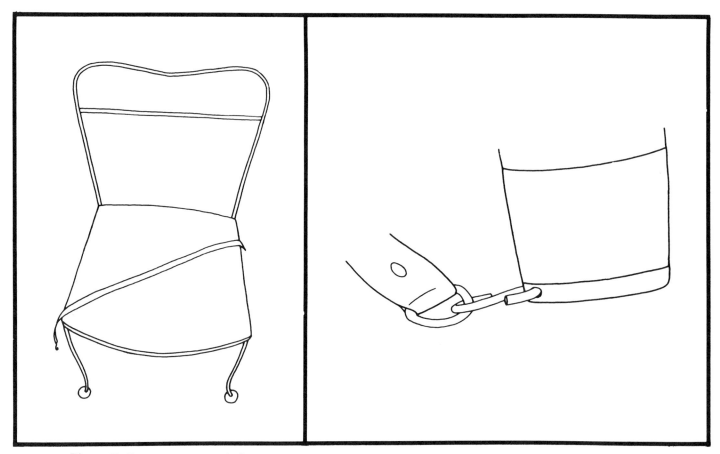

Figure 7. Seatstrap across chair   Figure 8. Hook into Boot Joint Cap.

Note: Bassoons without a hole in the Boot Joint cap can either have one drilled or have a small eyelet silver-soldered to the cap by a competent repair person. Commercial adapters also can be used.

There are many types of commercial seatstraps available. It is also easy to make a strap by tying a hook from a neckstrap into one of the holes from an old leather belt. The buckle and tapered end must be cut off (Figure 9).

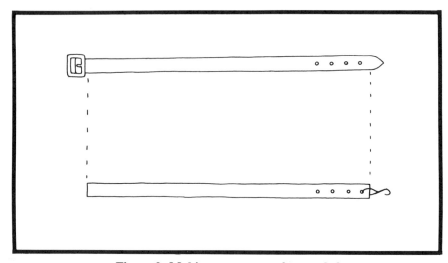

Figure 9. Making a seatstrap from a belt.

Playing Position

1. Sit to the *right of the chair* so that the bassoon rests against the right thigh. The bassoon should never touch the seat of the chair (Figure 10).

2. Adjust the seatstrap so that the bocal comes into the mouth without having to either raise or lower the head. The bassoon must come to you—not you to the bassoon! The seatstrap can be adjusted by pulling the strap with the left hand and positioning the bassoon with the right hand.

3. The left elbow remains close to the side but not touching and the bassoonist looks to the right side of the bassoon to read the music (Figure 11). If it is necessary to stand to play (the *National Anthem*, for instance), a neckstrap must be used.

Figure 10. Playing Position (Front)   **Figure 11. Playing Position (Rear)**

Hand Position

1. The left-hand fingers are slightly curved and the tone holes are covered with the balls or pads of the fingers—not the fingertips.
2. The left thumb "hovers" over the Whisper Key (Figure 12).
3. The right-hand thumb "hovers" over the Low E Key (Pancake Key) where it can easily move to either the B♭ or F♯ keys when needed. Do not rest the thumb on the metal band (ferrule) at the top of the boot joint. (Figure 13).
4. The first finger of the right hand rests on the rod of the C♯ Trill Key and the little finger rests on the F Key.

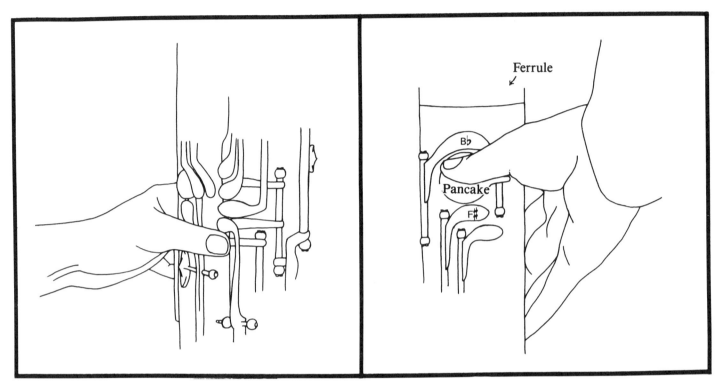

Figure 12. Left-Hand Position.   Figure 13. Right Hand Position.

Embouchure (Lip Formation)

The bassoon embouchure is an "overbite"—the upper jaw is over the lower jaw. Practice forming the embouchure with the reed alone as follows:

1. Place the reed on the lower lip (Figure 14).
2. Draw the reed into the mouth and take the lower lip with it (Figure 15).
3. With the top lip curved lightly over the top teeth, bring the top lip down (Figure 16). The top lip comes almost to the wire.

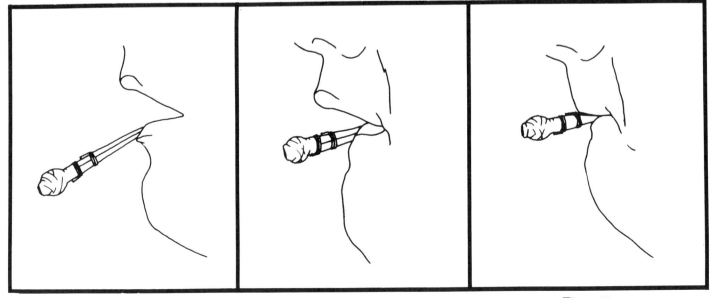

Figure 14.
Reed on lower lip.

Figure 15.
Reed into mouth with lower lip.

Figure 16.
Top lip comes down.

10

Since everyone's lips are different, the embouchure concept should not be seen as absolute. People with "fat" or heavy lips will have to adjust so that less lip will be taken into the mouth; people with the upper lip away from the teeth will find it difficult to "overlap." The embouchure presented here is for the person with "normal" structure. When necessary, adaptations may have to be made to take the individual into account.

Many students never put enough reed into the mouth. The embouchure is basically a "pucker" formation of the lips with a slight "smile" from the bottom. Notes that use the least number of fingers need the most bottom lip pressure, but it is never excessive.

Blowing on the reed alone produces a "crow" sound. This is really a multi-voice sound which should have low, middle, and high pitches. If the reed only crows with a single pitch or just a few tones, the embouchure may be too tight or pinched or the reed may be of poor quality or in need of adjustment. Quite often, the reed itself is incapable of producing the "crow" sound. Never pinch the reed with the lips.

Reeds

The best bassoon reeds are those made *by hand* by a bassoonist. Procuring reeds from a professional bassoonist and/or bassoon teacher is the best solution for the beginning student. Eventually, after you have had some time to practice the instrument and learn what to look for in a good reed, you can begin to learn how to make your own reeds. In the beginning, obtain the best reeds you can and begin to learn how a good reed sounds and "feels." Then, when you are ready to begin reedmaking lessons, you will have a "standard" in your mind. Many people learn to "compensate" on bad reeds—but compensating is not what good bassoon playing is all about. If you have no source for reeds, write to the publisher for a current listing of bassoon reed sources.

Careful construction and proper dimensions are essential for a well-playing reed. The most important aspect, though, is the "trim" of the reed—the wood that is carefully and skillfully scraped from the blades of the reed with a knife, files, and sandpaper. This is strictly a "hand" operation and a good trim will make the difference between a reed that plays and one that plays well. When you hold the reed up to a strong light, you should see the "heart" of the reed (Figure 17). The "heart" is the heavy area in the center. The reed is thinner on the sides and at the tip (Figure 18). The dimensions of the reed are given below. While these dimensions are approximate and may vary slightly from reedmaker to reedmaker, these are the standard dimensions and your reed should not deviate from these by any extreme.

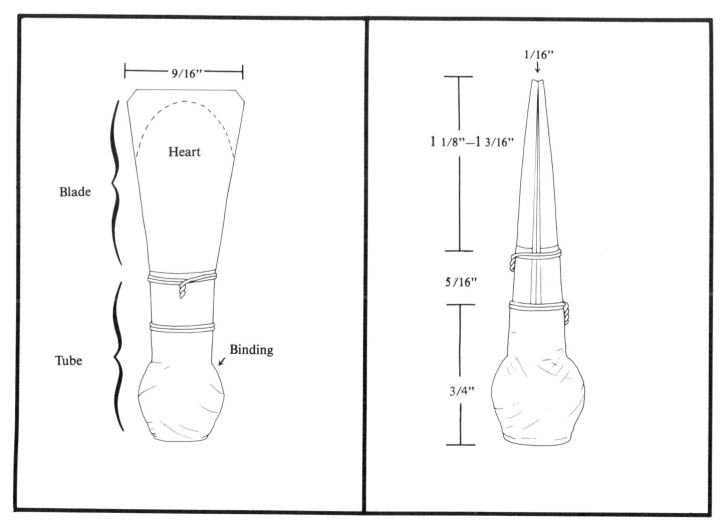

Figure 17. Reed (front).   **Figure 18. Reed (side).**

You must soak the reed in water for a few minutes before beginning to play. The reed should be completely water-proof at the binding so the entire reed can be placed in the water. If you hear a "hissing" or "bubbling" sound when you play, that means that the reed tube is larger than the bocal. Just lick around the base of the reed while it is on the bocal—the saliva will seal any leaks present (Figure 19).

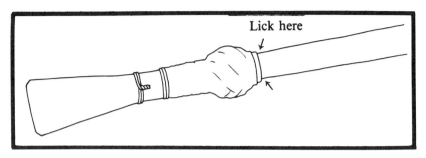

Figure 19. Sealing the reed on the bocal.

Every reed has a "good side" and a "bad side." The good side always goes on top (facing the ceiling). The reed-maker should mark the top side. If your reed is not marked, play the reed on both sides and decide which side is better—which side allows you to play softly, in tune, etc. As you become experienced, you will learn ways to determine the best side of a reed.

Never store reeds in the airtight containers in which they are often shipped or sold. Store the reed in a container that will allow it to dry. A commercial reed case is excellent, but not necessary. A small box lined with tissue works well. Metal lozenge or metal cigarette boxes are recommended. When you have finished playing, blow hard through the tube (bottom) end. Saliva will be blown out onto the blades of the reed. Wipe each blade off on the palm of the hand and place it in the box.

Breathing

Always breathe from the top lip. The bottom lip always stays in contact with the reed. The breath must be taken from the diaphragm area (Figure 20). The diaphragm is a muscle that moves in and out. As it moves inward, the air is directed upward. This is the most natural way to breathe—it is the way one breathes when sleeping. To experience diaphragmatic breathing, sit in a chair in a "doubled-over" position (Figure 21) and take a breath. This is the way the breath must feel when playing a wind instrument. If your shoulders move up and down as you play, you are not breathing from the diaphragm.

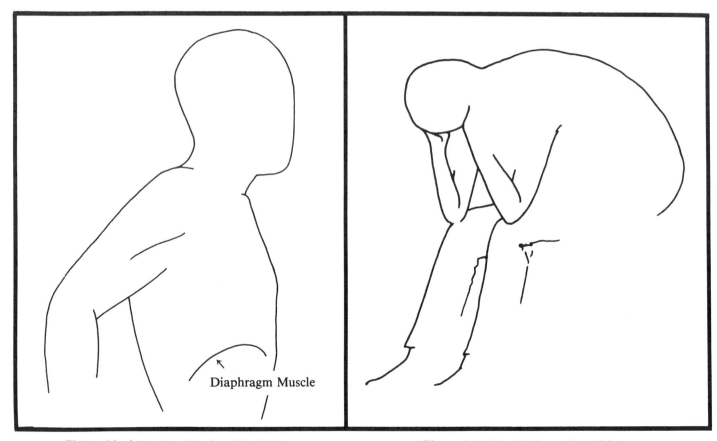

Figure 20. Anatomy showing Diaphragm   **Figure 21. "Doubled-over" position**

Cleaning the Bassoon

To understand how to clean the bassoon after playing, it is important to know something about the instrument's construction. The Wing Joint is lined with hard rubber. The Boot Joint has two holes bored through its entire length—the smaller of these holes is also lined with hard rubber while the larger hole is unlined. Both the Bass Joint and the Bell are not lined. As the bassoon is played, small amounts of saliva run down through the bocal and into the Wing Joint and then into the small bore of the Boot Joint. The water then settles and collects in the metal U-Tube that connects the two sides of the Boot Joint (Figure 22).

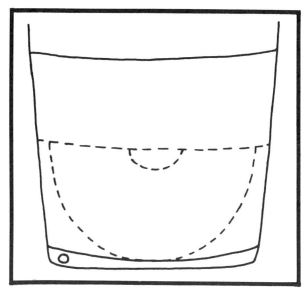

Figure 22. U-Tube under Boot Joint Cap

Once you start to play, the *bassoon must not be lowered horizontally* (i.e., on the floor, across a chair, across the lap while marking music, etc.) or the accumulated water will run up the side of the boot joint that is unlined. This will cause the wood, over a period of time, to rot! When you are finished playing, clean your bassoon using the following steps:

1. Twist out the bocal and blow the water out. Place the bocal in the case.
2. Keeping the bassoon in an up-and-down position, take off the Bell and Bass Joint and lay them in the case. They do not need to be swabbed.
3. Twist out the Wing Joint and set it aside to clean later. Pour the water out of the *small side* of the Boot (the smaller of the two holes). A cotton cloth swab attached to a metal cleaning rod is recommended for swabbing the Boot Joint (Figure 23). Avoid swabs on wooden handles which are full of lint and really do not absorb moisture well. Move the swab up and down a few times, but never "jam" the swab through to the bottom as you could puncture the delicate U-Tube. With the swab still in the bore, blow the water out of the two finger holes and *also out of the C♯ Trill pad* (see Fingering Chart). Water accumulates in this C♯ hole and eventually drips to the bottom of the boot. There is no need to swab out the large side of the Boot Joint.
4. A pull-through type swab is recommended to clean the Wing Joint. There are two types: one is pulled all the way through and the other is only pulled through until some resistance is felt and then drawn back through the original end. The latter type is preferred as it is the "safest" if used properly. If the pull-through type would break inside the bore, removal would be a job for a professional repair person. When swabbing out the Wing Joint, be sure to blow the water out of the three finger holes.

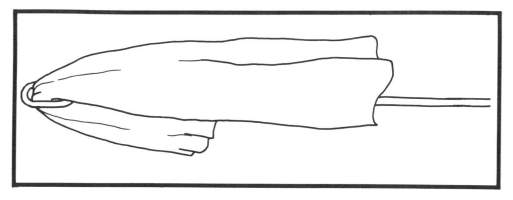

Figure 23. Swab and Metal Rod

Tips on Care

1. Do not "lock" the Bass Joint and the Wing Joint together while they are in the case. If the bassoon case were to be dropped or bumped, the joint lock could be torn off.

2. Do not keep a bassoon in a hot automobile trunk; heat is not good for the wood. Remember, the trunk gets much hotter than the rest of the car. Also, many bassoons have a coating of paraffin wax on the pads. The heat could melt this wax.

3. Put the bassoon in the case when not in use.

4. The bassoon should not move around in the case. Where there are "spaces" between the case blockings and the bassoon sections, fill these spaces with pieces of towel or heavy cloth. If the blockings themselves are loose, have the case repaired. Never store music in the bassoon case. The additional bulk could cause the delicate keywork to bend.

5. When walking with an assembled bassoon, place the bocal in the Bell so the cork end of the bocal sticks out. In playing position, the bocal is too vulnerable.

6. The keywork should be oiled once every six (6) weeks. DO NOT OVER OIL. A toothpick works very well as a small dropper. A *small drop* of high-grade oil (woodwind key oil, sewing machine oil, watch oil) is put in all the connections where metal touches metal.

7. It is not usually necessary to oil the bore of the bassoon as the wood is usually treated in oil for many years in the course of manufacturing. If the wood does become excessively dry, however, have a technician treat the unlined sections of the bore with *raw* linseed oil for about twenty (20) minutes. Do not soak in oil for an extended period of time.

8. When you are finished playing, wipe off the keywork with a soft cloth—especially the keys touched by the fingers. This will help keep the finish/plating bright. Silver-plated keys resist tarnish; nickel keywork will eventually tarnish. A soft paintbrush (one inch) is excellent to remove dust from under the keys.

9. If your bassoon is made from wood, the wood may "shrink" slightly during the colder weather and "expand" a little during the warmer months. When the wood shrinks, the tenons may not fit tightly. To remedy this, take some *cotton* thread and wrap some around the cork on the loose tenon or add some to a threaded tenon. When the warmer weather comes, simply remove the "winter thread."

Additional Materials

Upon completion of PRIMARY HANDBOOK FOR BASSOON, the following studies are recommended:

Studies for Advanced Students by Julius Weissenborn, Edited by Simon Kovar, Volume II (International)

25 Studies in Scales & Chords, Op. 24 by L. Milde, Edited by Simon Kovar (International)

30 Concert Studies, Op. 26 by L. Milde, Edited by Simon Kovar (International)

Difficult Passages and Solos for Bassoon (Orchestral Excerpts) by Ciro Stadio (Ricordi)

The following books on bassoon reedmaking are recommended:

Bassoon Reedmaking by Mark Popkin and Loren Glickman (published by *The Instrumentalist*, Evanston, Il.)

Bassoon Reed-Making: A Basic Technique by Chris Weait (McGinnis & Marx, New York)

The following book on bassoon fingerings is recommended:

Essentials of Bassoon Technique by Lewis Hugh Cooper and Howard Toplansky (Published by Howard Toplansky, 559 Winthrop Rd., Union, New Jersey 07083)

The following books are recommended for information on bassoon technique, performance and history:

The Art of Bassoon Playing by William Spencer (Summy-Birchard)

Bassoon Technique by Archie Camden (Oxford University Press)

The Bassoon and Double Bassoon by Lyndesay Langwill (Hinrichsen Edition, Ltd.)

The Bassoon by Wilhelm Heckel (Jack Spratt Woodwind Publications, Old Greenwich, Conn.)

New Notes

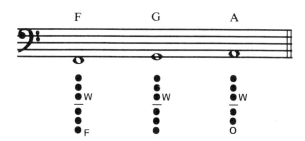

Note: The third "finger hole" for the right hand is really *not* a tone hole on the bassoon! It is actually the G Key (see Fingering Chart).

Performance Techniques

To "Tongue" (or start) the tone:
1. Place the tip of the tongue on the tip of the reed.
2. Blow the air against the reed.
3. Pull back the tongue while saying "tah."

IMPORTANT: The breath is taken from the *top lip only*—the bottom lip always stays on the reed.

Key of F

Take a breath on each quarter rest.

A comma (,) indicates a place for a breath.

Instrument Check

Depress the whisper key. The whisper key pad should come *all the way* to the vent on the side of the bocal and completely cover the small hole of this vent. If it does not, take the instrument to a bassoon technician for adjustment.

Performance Techniques

IMPORTANT: Make sure the tone holes are covered with the balls of the fingers (fleshy part)—not the fingertips. A "squawk," multi-pitch sound, is caused when the tone hole is not *completely* covered. Finger G and then press hard with your fingers. Take your left hand away and look at the balls of the fingers—you should see the "full circle" impression of the tone holes. Repeat with the right hand.

Music Fundamentals

"C" stands for Common Meter. It is the same as $\frac{4}{4}$.

Music Fundamentals—Dynamics

fortissimo (ff)	=	very loud
forte *(f)*	=	loud
mezzo forte *(mf)*	=	moderately loud
mezzo piano *(mp)*	=	moderately soft
piano *(p)*	=	soft
pianissimo *(pp)*	=	very soft

16

New Note

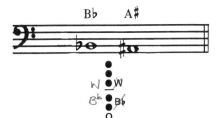

This note has the same fingering as Low A but with the addition of the B♭ Key depressed by the right thumb.

The second beat does not end until the third beat begins.

Performance Techniques

Make sure the right-hand thumb "hovers" over the Low E Key (the round key which is often called the "Pancake Key"). This makes the distance to the B♭ Key short and within easy reach. Do not rest the thumb on the metal at the top of the boot joint.

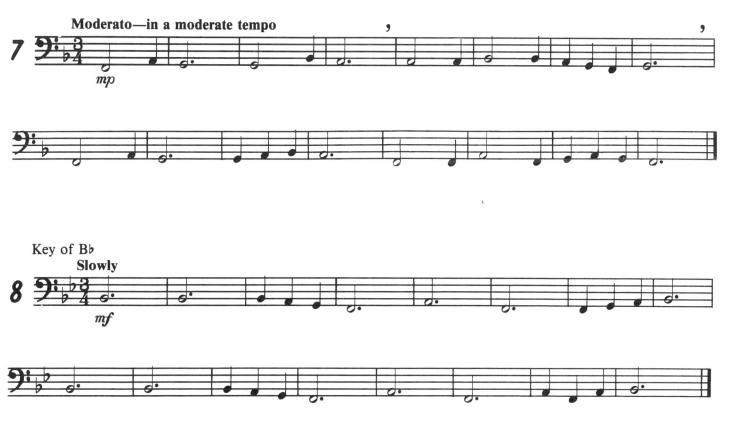

Music Fundamentals

A "tie" is a curved line joining two notes of the same pitch which will be sounded as one note equal to their combined time value. (♩ ♩ = ♩ or ♩ ♩ = ♩.)

The final measure of number ten (10) has only five beats. The last beat is used to begin the music. This beginning note is call an "Anacrusis" (sometimes called a "pick-up" note).

New Note

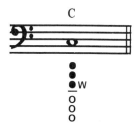

This note uses only the left hand. Keep the right hand in the proper position—thumb hovers over Low E Key, first and second fingers are kept close to the tone holes, the third finger over the G Key, and the little finger over the F Key.

Music Fundamentals

Slur—a curved line connecting two or more notes of different pitch is called a slur. Only the first note is tongued. This is also called "legato" style, which means smooth and connected with no break between the tones.

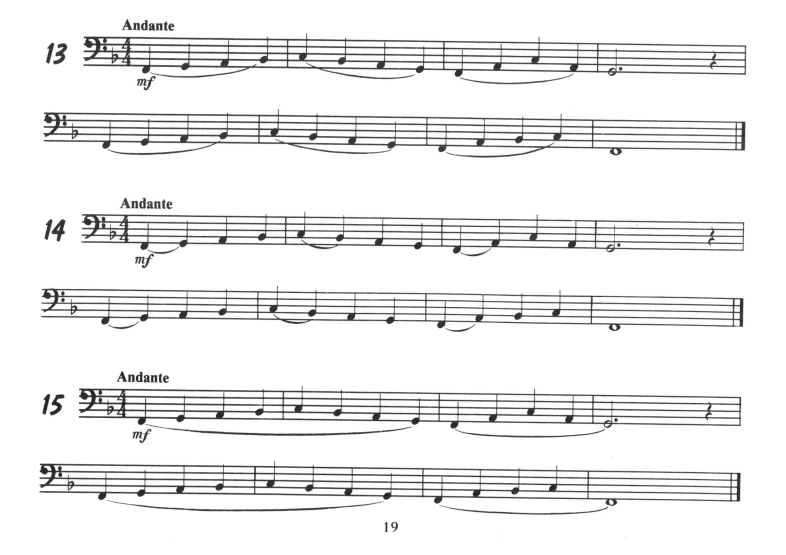

New Notes

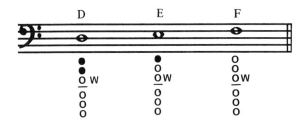

Performance Techniques

Notes with fewer tone holes covered have a tendency to "sink" or to go flat. As fewer tone holes are used, add a *little* pressure *from the bottom lip only*. Of the above notes, F will have the most "bottom lip" pressure because it has the fewest covered holes.

Lightly Row

New Note

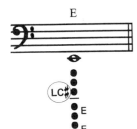

It is not necessary to use the Whisper Key when playing Low E because it goes down automatically when the Low E Key (Pancake Key) is depressed; however, the Whisper Key is often held down anyway as it is the best place for the thumb to rest. The Low C♯ Key may be added to this note *if needed* to improve resonance and/or intonation and to aid in playing softly. This key should only be added if it does not cause technical difficulty.

Largo

Key of C
Moderato

America

CAREY

Maestoso—majestically, dignified

Instrument Check

Depress the Low E Key. Now look at the Whisper Key pad. It should fully cover the vent on the bocal. If it doesn't, the instrument is out of adjustment and should be regulated by a bassoon technician. This "leak" will make all notes from Low E down difficult to sound.

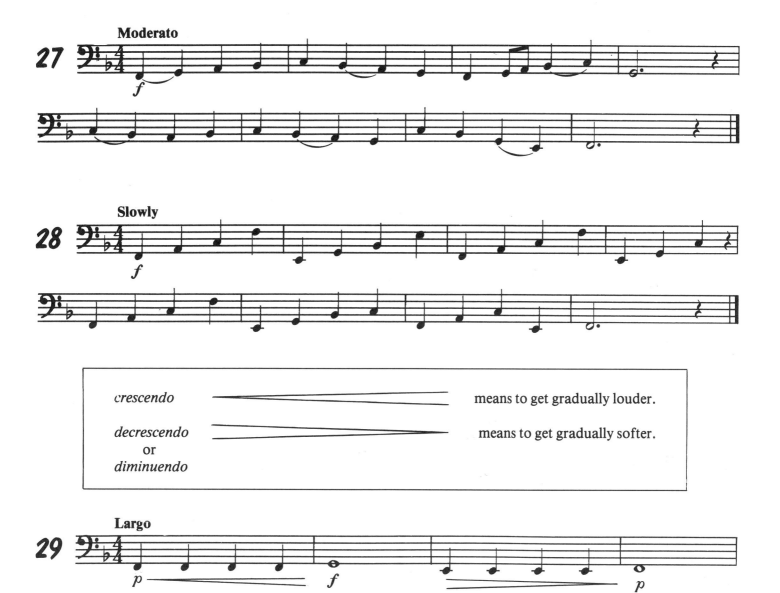

Music Fundamentals

A *fermata (⌢),* or "hold" in English, above or below a note means to hold that note longer than the printed value.

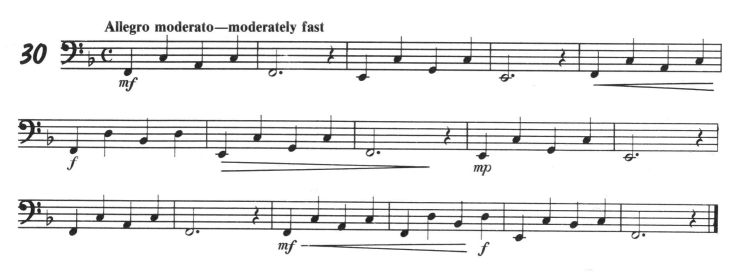

New Notes

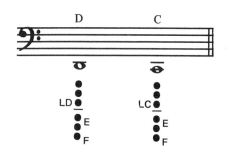

LOW D— The Low D Key is not fingered with the tip of the thumb as the Whisper Key is. To achieve the correct position, place the thumb on the Whisper Key. While holding the tip of the thumb on the Whisper Key, depress the Low D Key with the back of the thumb. This is where the thumb hits Low D.

LOW C—Like Low D, the Low C Key is depressed with the back part of the thumb. In going from D to C, the thumb *slides* to the C Key.

Performance Techniques

Think "ah" for the lowest notes. That syllable makes the throat larger and will help the low register to be in tune.

Instrument Check

Depress the Low D Key and watch the pad go down. While watching this pad, slide to the Low C Key—the pad should stay down. If it moves up, the instrument will leak from Low C down. If needed, have a bassoon technician adjust the instrument.

New Note

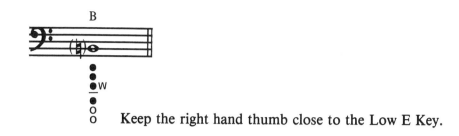

Keep the right hand thumb close to the Low E Key.

33

Music Fundamentals

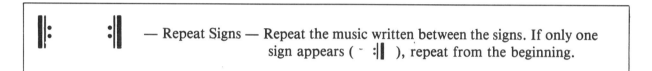

— Repeat Signs — Repeat the music written between the signs. If only one
sign appears (‖: :‖), repeat from the beginning.

34

Music Fundamentals

An accent mark (>) above or below the note means to accent or stress the note.

35

New Note

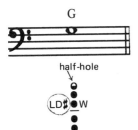

G

half-hole

The fingering for this G is similar to the Low G fingering. The first finger of the left hand only covers part of the hole, however. This is called the "half-hole." *If needed,* the Low D♯ Key may be added (unless the music is very fast and/or too technically difficult) to this basic fingering to correct the intonation and/or resonance of this note.

Performance Techniques

To find the correct size of the half-hole, play Low G and "slur" to the upper G by *rolling* the first finger down. As you roll, the exact place that the G jumps from low to high is the opening of the half-hole. **Always *roll* the finger to the "half-hole"—never pick the finger up and place it in position:**

Note: Practice this many times over several days. Soon your finger will "know" where the half-hole is all of the time.

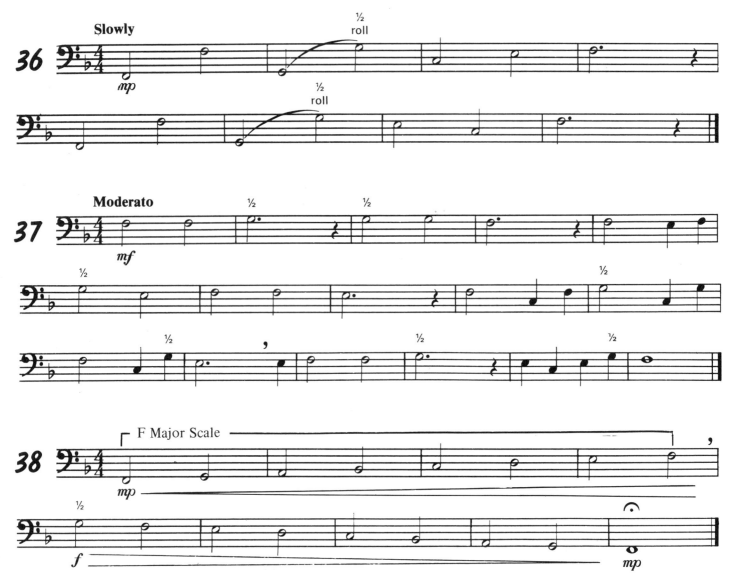

26

New Notes

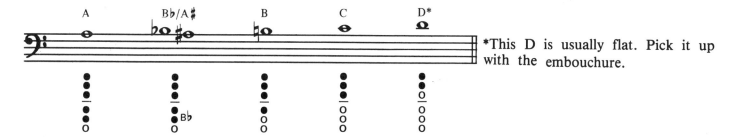

*This D is usually flat. Pick it up with the embouchure.

Performance Techniques

These notes are fingered exactly as an octave lower except that no Whisper Key is used. Think "e-e-e" rather than "ah-h-h" when playing these notes. They require more air support (diaphragmatic support) to stay in the higher octave. Also, keep the left thumb hovering over the Whisper Key so it will not have to travel far when needed later.

Instrument Check

If any of these new notes "growl" or will only sound in the low octave, the bocal vent may be clogged and/or dirty. Clean this small hole with a broom straw or single brush bristle. Do not clean with a pin.

Performance Techniques

When pick-up notes (Anacruses) occur within the music, always take the breath before the pick-up. Pick-up notes are circled below:

Marines' Hymn

OFFENBACH
from the opera *Genevieve de Brabant*

Hickory, Dickory Dock

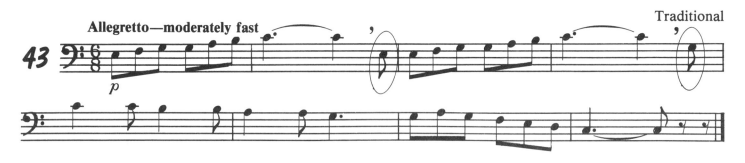

Traditional

Variation (an octave* lower)

Long Tones

It is a good idea to play some "Long Tones" every day to develop breath support and embouchure control. Can you play these notes and keep the tone steady for a full eight beats? Practice this exercise on other tones, too.

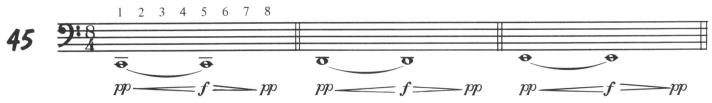

*An octave is the distance between eight tones—from C to C, D to D, etc.

New Notes

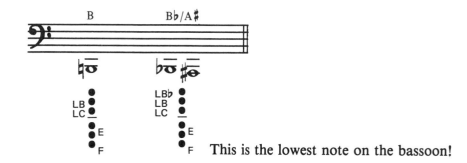

This is the lowest note on the bassoon!

Performance Techniques

When the Low B Key is depressed, the Low C Key automatically is depressed too. However, it is recommended that whenever this Low B Key is used, the Low C Key should also be held down with the thumb.

Don't forget to use your thumb on the Whisper Key (W.K.) for all the Low F's:

Instrument Check

The Low Bb Key and Low B Key spatulas (the part of the key pressed by the thumb) should be the same height—level with the Low C Spatula. If they are not, adjustment by a technician is needed.

New Note

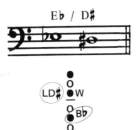

Eb / D#

The basic Eb fingering is the first and third fingers of the left hand and the Whisper Key. *If needed* (to correct possible instability and/or intonation), the Low D# Key can be added plus the second finger of the right hand with the Bb Key (right thumb). On some bassoons, the first finger of the right hand—instead of the second—may be better. On fast technical passages, use only the basic fingering.

Key of Eb Major

50 *mf*

51 Not too fast *f*

Music Fundamentals

Accidentals are sharps, flats or naturals which occur within the music and temporarily alter the pitch of notes. An accidental affects the note immediately following it, and remains valid for all the notes of the same pitch (but not in different octaves) *within that measure only*.

C Minor

52 *mf*

Music Fundamentals

First and Second Endings: Play the 1st ending the first time through and repeat the strain. The second time through skip the 1st ending, play the 2nd ending, and go on.

Oh, Christmas Tree

German Folk Song

53 Moderato *mf*

New Notes

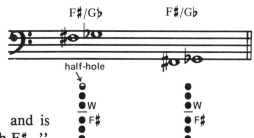

This is the basic fingering for F# and is sometimes referred to as "Thumb F#"

These notes have the same fingerings except for the "half-hole" in the upper octave. Practice slurring to find the correct position for the half-hole. Remember to *roll* the finger open.

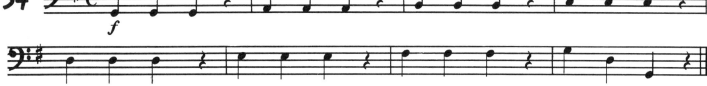

Music Fundamentals

A dot placed above or below a note indicates that the note is to be played *staccato*—detached and separated. A note marked staccato will usually be held for half of its printed value.

End the note staccato by placing the tongue back on the reed.

Practice this piece slowly—a measure at a time. Then work for speed.

Listen to Mozart's *Concerto for Piano and Orchestra #20*. This is one of the bassoon solos.

31

New Note

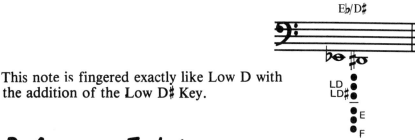

This note is fingered exactly like Low D with the addition of the Low D♯ Key.

Performance Techniques

Two Legato: Whenever notes are written "two legato" (two notes slurred), never accent the cut-off of the second note. In number fifty-seven (57), play the second note of each slur slightly shorter and softer than the first note.

Two Legato, Two Staccato: Whenever notes are written "two legato, two staccato" (two slurred, two tongued), never accent the second note of the slur. Play the second note of the slur slightly shorter and softer than the first note. This will prepare the subsequent staccato.

New Notes

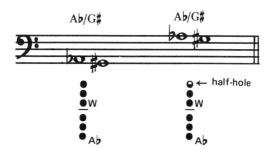

These notes have the same fingering except for the "half-hole" in the upper octave. Practice slurring to find the correct finger position for the half-hole. Remember to *roll* the finger open.

Music Fundamentals

Sempre means "always" or "continually." In Exercise 63, play all the notes staccato.

Instrument Check

Finger Low F and slide the right hand little finger to the A♭ Key. The finger should not "get stuck" between the keys. Now slide from A♭ back to F. Again, the slide should be very smooth. Now slide F to A♭ to Alternate F♯. The little finger should be able to make a "full circle" without getting stuck on any key. If needed, have a bassoon technician regulate these keys.

New Note

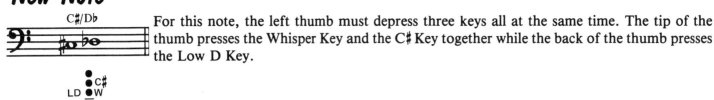

For this note, the left thumb must depress three keys all at the same time. The tip of the thumb presses the Whisper Key and the C♯ Key together while the back of the thumb presses the Low D Key.

Smoothly

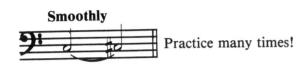

Practice many times!

Instrument Check

Depress the C♯ Key. This opens the C♯ pad at the end of this key. It should also make the "ring" over the third finger hole come up in addition to raising the small pad to the upper right of the C♯ pad. This is called the B Resonance pad. Now, while holding down the C♯, close the ring by covering the third tone hole. This should close the B Resonance pad, too. If this mechanism does not operate as described, have it adjusted by a technician.

Music Fundamentals

D.C. al Fine: Means to repeat from the beginning (*D.C.—Da Capo:* "from the head") and play to the *fine,* ("the end").

Twinkle, Twinkle Little Star

Music Fundamentals

Triplet: A group of three equal notes to be played in the time it would take to play *two of these notes.*

An eighth-note triplet  is played in the time of two eighth notes 𝅘𝅥𝅮𝅘𝅥𝅮.

Number 68 could have been written in $\frac{2}{4}$ time using triplets:

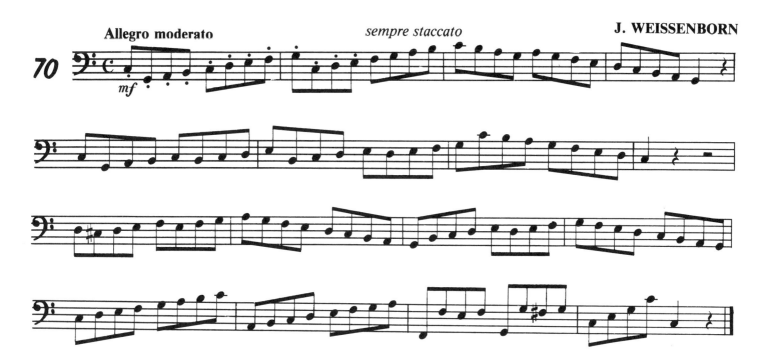

New Note

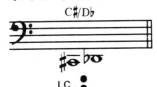

This note is fingered exactly like Low C with the addition of the Low C♯ Key depressed by the little finger of the left hand. Make sure the Low C Key is depressed with the *back* part of the thumb.

Music Fundamentals

A Chromatic Scale ascends (goes up) or descends (goes down) by half steps. There are thirteen tones in a Chromatic Scale

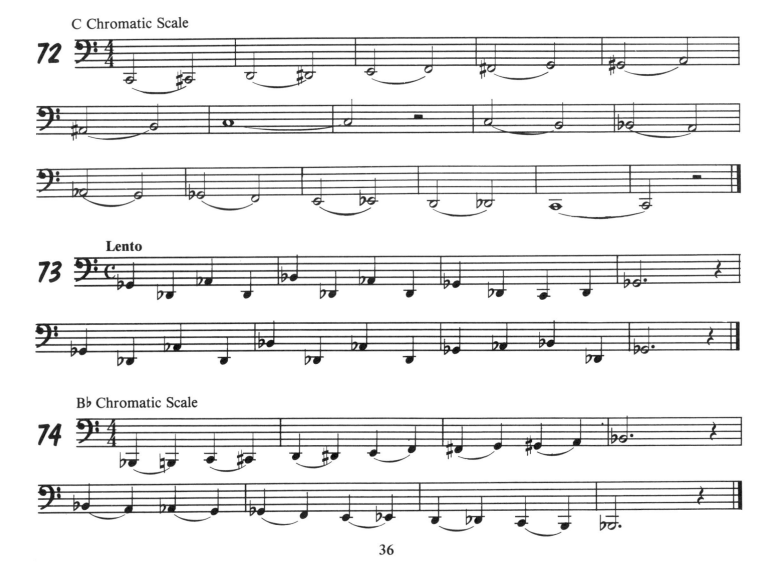

Music Fundamentals

Portamento: Notes with dots and a slur ♩̣ ♩̣ ♩̣ ♩̣ are to be played *portamento*—very lightly tongued with little space between the notes. The tongue should touch the reed with the syllable "dah" instead of "tah."

Instrument Check

If you hear a "gurgle" sound as you play, there is water in one of the five tone holes. This water can be blown out of the holes to stop the gurgling. However, it may not be necessary to blow into all five holes. It is only necessary to blow into those holes *not covered* on the note in question. The arrows indicate which holes must be blown into:

Note: Blow very hard into the tone holes so all the water is blown back into the bassoon's bore. When doing this, be very careful not to bump the reed against you, the music stand, etc.

New Note

The basic fingering for this note is shown on the left. An alternate fingering that is more resonant and that emphasizes the tenor quality of the bassoon is called the "Long C♯," shown on the right. This has a tendency to be slightly sharp. Think "low" when using this alternate fingering.

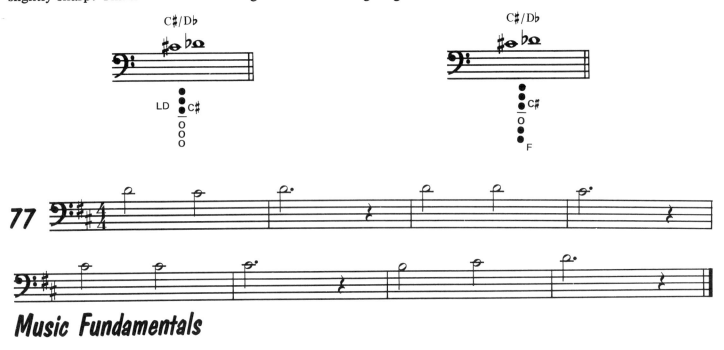

Music Fundamentals

A Repeat Sign ⁒ in a measure means to repeat the previous measure.

Music Fundamentals

¢ stands for *alla breve*. It is the same as $\frac{2}{2}$.

Don Giovanni Overture

MOZART

Practice this passage from the overture to *Don Giovanni* very slowly and gradually increase your speed.

New Note

Alternate F♯/G♭

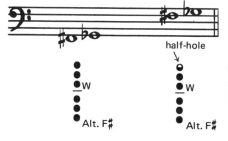

This alternate fingering for F♯/G♭ is used when going to or counting from any note which uses the thumb B♭ Key.

The Alternate F♯ Key is depressed by the little finger of the right hand. The F Key automatically goes down when the F♯ Key is depressed. Do not press both Keys down—only the F♯ Key.

In this text, an asterik (*) will be used to indicate the use of the alternate F♯. You might want to use this symbol to mark your music.

81

Practice examples (A), (B), and (C) many times. First, tongue each note. Then slur two notes making sure the fingers change smoothly. Then, slur four notes.

Note: the fingering for C♭ is the same as B♮.

Instrument Check

The Alternate F♯ Key should open slightly (one millimeter) before the F Key goes down with it. This is called having "play" in the key. If there is no play in this key, have a technician adjust the instrument.

New Note

This is the basic fingering for this note. *If needed,* the Low D♯ Key can be added for increased resonance and/or to correct intonation.

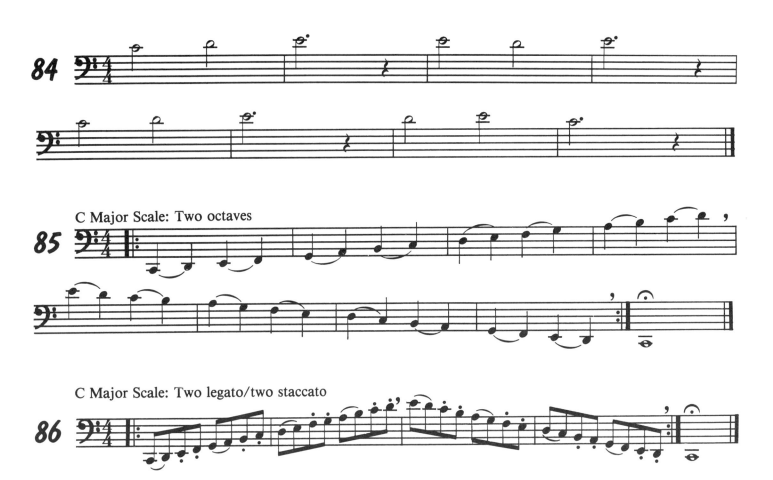

84

85 C Major Scale: Two octaves

86 C Major Scale: Two legato/two staccato

Music Fundamentals

D.S. 𝄋 *al Coda* ⊕ means repeat to the 𝄋 *(D.S.—Dal Segno:* "to the sign"); when you reach ⊕, skip to the *Coda* which is a short concluding section.

87 **Presto—fast, rapid**

f

𝄋

D.S. 𝄋 *al coda* ⊕.

mp

⊕ *Coda*

f   *p*

New Note

F

This fingering is exactly like high E except that the third finger of the right hand (G Key) is up. This is the basic fingering for this note. *If needed,* the Low D# Key can be added for increased resonance and/or to correct intonation.

88 Slowly

89

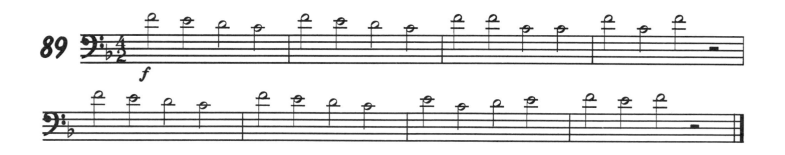

J. WEISSENBORN

90 Moderato

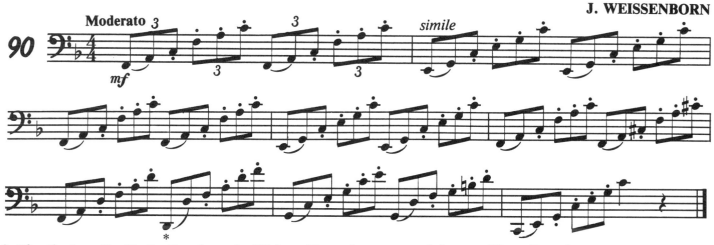

* Play the Low D with the thumb on the Whisper Key—then you won't have to "jump" to the next note.

Finale–Symphony No. 4

TSCHAIKOWSKY

91

New Note

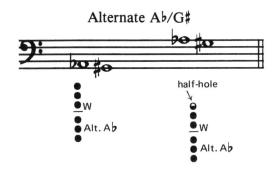

Alternate Ab/G♯

The Alternate Ab/G♯ fingering is used when the right hand little finger is coming from or going to the F Key when it is *technically awkward* to move the little finger between the F and Ab Keys. The Alternate Ab Key is depressed with the right hand thumb. Except for the half-hole, the octaves are fingered the same. Many times, it will be easier to "slide" F to Ab with the little finger. Use the alternate only when necessary.

Practice this excerpt from the *Danzi Woodwind Quintet* very slowly and then work for speed.

Quintet, Op. 56, No. 2

DANZI

Instrument Check

Depress the Ab Key and look at the wood under the pad. It should be the same color as the wood under the other pads. If it is very dark and/or the finish is gone or the pad itself is dark, hard and brittle, there is rotting taking place in the bottom of the boot joint. On some bassoons, the Alternate Ab Key opens this same pad, however, on other bassoons, a different pad opens on the opposite side of the boot. Check this pad and the wood under it. Rotting can be corrected by a bassoon technician. Rotting *can be prevented* by following the cleaning instructions in the Introduction.

Music Fundamentals

The Relative Minor Scale begins on the sixth tone of the Major Scale:

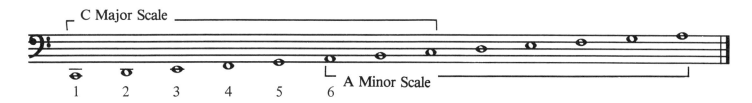

Thus, the Relative Minor for C Major is A Minor. They are termed "relative" because they are related by a common key signature. There are three types of Minor Scales:

Natural Minor: uses the same notes and key signature as the Major but starts on the sixth degree of the scale.

Harmonic Minor: the seventh tone of the scale is raised a half (½) step.

Melodic Minor: The sixth and seventh tones are raised ascending; played as natural minor scale descending.

A minor: Natural—two legato

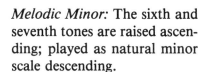

A minor: Harmonic—two legato

A minor: Melodic—two legato

D minor: Harmonic—two legato

New Note

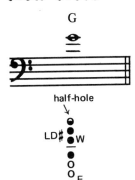

Do not pinch the reed when playing in the high register; instead, use more support or "push" from the diaphragm. The reed must vibrate faster as you play higher. Pinching the reed would be counter productive. For high G, make sure you use the Whisper Key and add the Low D♯ Key for proper resonance and intonation.

Don't pinch! Think "e-e-e" in the high register.

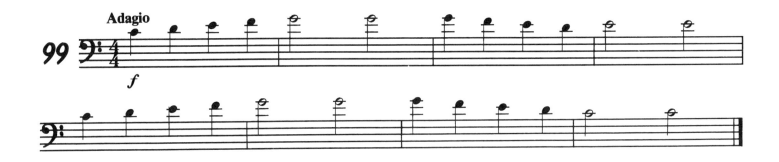

Performance Techniques

When playing two legato, one staccato, the second note is slightly shorter and softer than the first note. This allows for "space" on both sides of the staccato note.

F Major—Two legato, one staccato

Instrument Check

On the boot joint, depress the Low F Key. The "ring" around the second tone hole should come up as well as the small pad directly above this tone hole. If it does not come up, the high G will not be correctly voiced or in tune. Next, hold the F Key down and depress the "ring" a few times. It should go down easily and "fly" right back up as the finger is released. Also, the tube that the "ring" goes around should not extend past the ring itself. The tube should be slightly lower than the ring key. If this mechanism is out of adjustment, take the instrument to a bassoon technician.

Performance Techniques

Sometimes it is necessary to alter the high E fingering when slurring to that note. For example, play the slur G to high E:

Notice how the E either does not speak or is very "hesitant" in speaking. To facilitate any slur to E which does not speak immediately, finger the high E without the first finger of the right hand:

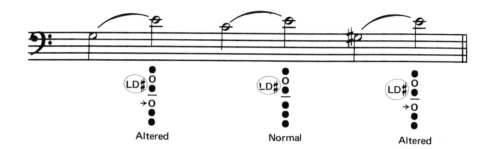

In the first measure of number 101, keep the left hand fingers in place and make the slur by changing the right hand fingers only. Keep the left hand the same for both notes:

New Note

Eb/D#

Do not use the Low D# Key on Eb/D#!

103

104 Eb Major—Two legato

105 Allegretto—quite lively, moderately fast

Overture Der Freischutz

C.M. VON WEBER

106 Molto vivace—very fast

dolce (sweetly)

Performance Techniques

"Flicking" is a technique used in playing the bassoon when slurring to these notes  from any note in the range: "Flicking" overcomes the danger of the slur accidentally dropping to the lower octave.

On the Wing Joint, the High A Key, the High C Key, and on those bassoons having it, the High D Key are additionally used as "flick" keys. To "flick" a key means to *lightly open it for just a split second* with the left thumb. The key is never fully depressed—just opened for an instant with the upward motion of the thumb. In this text, a plus sign (+) is used to indicate a note to be flicked.

"Flick" keys on bassoons without the High D Key.   "Flick" keys on bassoons with the High D Key.

Example: In the following slur, the A Key will be "flicked" by the left thumb at the exact moment that the fingers change from E to A. Be careful not to fully depress the A Key. It just opens for an instant.

Here is an exercise to learn the technique of "flicking." Practice this exercise *very* slowly.

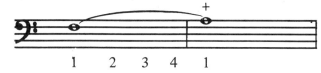

Measure 1, Beat 1 — Play Low A
Beat 2 — Whisper Key up
Beat 3 — Left thumb travels upward to "flick" key (High A Key)
Beat 4 — Left thumb lands on "flick" key
Measure 2, Beat 1 — "Flick" High A Key

Now try this one in which the fingerings change.

Measure 1, Beat 1 — Play E
Beat 2 — Whisper Key up
Beat 3 — Left thumb travels upward to "flick" key (High A Key)
Beat 4 — Left thumb lands on "flick" key
Measure 2, Beat 1 — Fingers change to A/left thumb "flicks" High A Key

Practice the following slurs very slowly. Be sure to "flick" with the correct key.

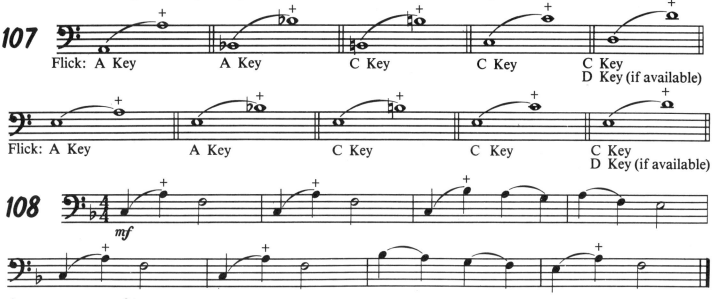

Instrument Check

The pads on the High A, High C, and High D Keys should be made out of cork instead of leather. Most bassoons are factory equipped with leather pads on these keys. Because the vents that they cover collect moisture, leather pads make a "popping" sound as they come up. Since cork is resistant to moisture, the cork pad is silent. The pads can be easily replaced by a technician.

Music Fundamentals

Transposition: Writing the same melody from one key to another is called transposition. Number 109 is the same melody as number 108. It is *transposed* from the key of F Major to the key of G Major.

*No "flick" is necessary from F♯ to B; only notes from F♮ and below.

Concert Studies, No. 41

New Note

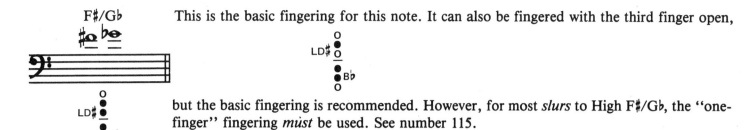

F♯/G♭

This is the basic fingering for this note. It can also be fingered with the third finger open, but the basic fingering is recommended. However, for most *slurs* to High F♯/G♭, the "one-finger" fingering *must* be used. See number 115.

113

f

Do not pinch the reed!

114

D Major Scale—Two legato

Music Fundamentals

The symbol // (*luftpause*) means to break or pause in the music. In the first full measure, if the "B" does not speak well in the slur, "flick" it.

J. WEISSENBORN

115

mf

mp

3

49

Common Trills for Bassoon

An arrow (→) indicates the "triller."

*(1) Bassoons without the D♯trill key can trill with the thumb C♯ key instead, with no Whisper Key on either note.

(2) With this fingering, there will be no Whisper Key on the F.

(trills continued)

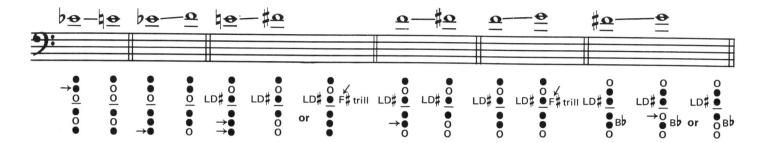

Performance Techniques

Some fingerings to play notes very "softly":

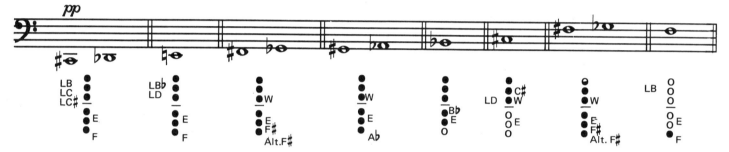

Instrument Check

A Whisper Key Lock is recommended to be added to bassoons without one. When the lock is "on", the thumb does not have to depress the Whisper Key as it is permanently closed until the lock is "off." Fast, technical passages in the low register are made much simpler:

(No W.K. on Low F!)

A technician can easily install the lock on bassoons not having one. They come in either right- or left-hand types. Most Americans prefer the right-hand type.

Music Fundamentals—Major and Minor Key Signatures

Major:	C	G	D	A	E	B	F♯	C♯
Minor:	a	e	b	f♯	c♯	g♯	d♯	a♯

Major:	F	B♭	E♭	A♭	D♭	G♭	C♭
Minor:	d	g	c	f	b♭	e♭	a♭

Music Fundamentals

To avoid using too many ledger lines when writing in the high register of the bassoon, composers often write these high notes in the *tenor clef*.

Middle C in the bass clef is located on the fourth line in the tenor clef. While it is recommended to learn to read the clef, the following "transposition chart" will clarify the bass-to-tenor relationship.

 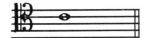

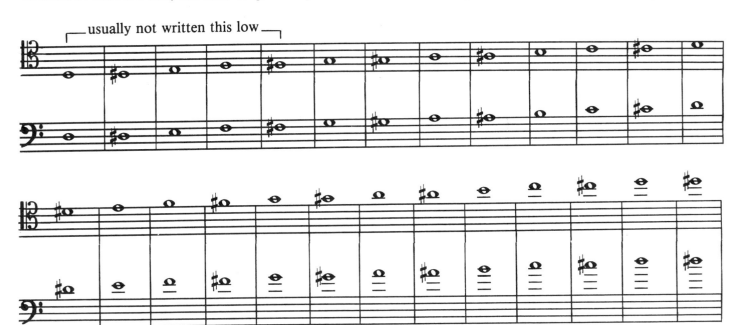

This is number 98 as it would look written in tenor clef (see page 44).

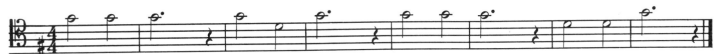

Number 99 written in tenor clef.

Number 106 written in tenor clef (See page 46).

Overture Der Freischutz

C.M. VON WEBER

52